Heartbeats
and
Heartstrings

MARK BROOKS

Volume 1

Author's Other Works

2017 – Poems For A Princess

About The Author

I'm Mark from Wolverhampton, deep thinker, over-thinker and self-confessed failure at talking feelings/emotions tending to instead express them through my writing. Writing is my release, my way of expressing my feelings and emotions. Writing has always been a passion of mine ever since I was a young child and my late Mother is to thank for that. When I'm not writing or daydreaming, I can be found working in a Law Firm.

<u>FOREWORD</u>

Hello, well, here we are, here we go again! Two years later than planned but nevertheless book two is here.

As you may know from my first book "Poems for a Princess" I'm Mark Brooks or "Brooksie" to friends and this is my second book for the Princess, the follow up to "Poems for a Princess", this book is another book of poems but this time poems inspired by songs that remind me of the Princess ... Poems that were inspired by songs that make my heart race and beat, poems inspired by songs that pull at my heartstrings when I hear the song as it reminds me of the special girl I have written these for. I just hope she likes them and sees from them how I feel about her. I just want her to see how special she is, I hope they tell her how beautiful, how sweet, how lovely, how amazing I think she is.

Again, I thank you for purchasing my book and reading me pour my heart out, ... again! and I just hope you enjoy reading them.

Love and happiness to you all!

Mark

xx

<u>Dedication</u>

Heartbeats and Heartstrings is dedicated to the most beautiful, most sweetest, most loveliest, most kindest, most funniest, most amazing, most special girl that I have ever met … the Princess!

Princess, this is my second book for you following "Poems for a Princess", I hope you will "get it" from this book, how I really feel about you, the secret feelings I feel for you and have kept hidden, too afraid to tell you in person, face to face, how I really feel, for, I guess, fear of looking stupid or being rejected.

I'm hoping this works and you finally realise how I really feel and you finally realise that you are the Princess, you are the special girl that I have written these books for, dedicated to, and especially for you.

Princess – this book is especially for you – I hope you like it.

All my love.

Mark

xxx

Acknowledgements

I would like to thank all my friends and family for all their loving support and encouragement and whom have encouraged me to release this, book two, the follow up to "Poems for a Princess".

A big thank you to my best friend James Robins who has kindly designed the front and back cover for "Heartbeats and Heartstrings" and for all the times he has counselled and borrowed me his ear at my lowest points and picked me up and encouraged me, so thanks mate.

A massive thank you once again to all of you, the readers who have purchased this book and some of you whom I know also purchased book one "Poems for a Princess". Thank you for all your support.

And lastly but definitely not least, another big thank you to the inspiration, the reason behind the book, "the Princess", for if it wasn't for you making me feel the way I do, none of these poems would ever have existed, I hope the poems tell you how amazing, how beautiful, how special you truly are.

HEARTBEATS & HEARTSTRINGS

Contents

Intro Poem – Music

Music

Intro

This poem is an introductory poem to the book.

As this book of poems for the Princess is inspired by songs that remind me of her I thought I would write a poem about music in general. A poem about how for every feeling you can imagine, there is music for it, for example a certain song like in this case can make you think and remind you of that somebody special and the Princess is special. There can be songs that remind you of happy times and songs that remind you of sad times and so on and so forth.

The poems in this book are inspired by songs that remind me of the most beautiful, most sweetest, most loveliest, most kindest, funniest, most special girl that I have ever met, the Princess and this is my second book for her.

Anyway, here is the introductory poem titled "Music" about the different feelings and emotions that music can trigger and the memories that it can bring back.

Funny thing is music,

It has a habit of doing that trick,

You hear a lyric,

And you start to think,

Music triggers so many memories,

So many thoughts,

Memories of a loved one,

Memories of those who are gone,

Memories of the good times,

Memories of the bad times you thought you had
left behind,

Music can be pessimistic,

Music can be optimistic,

Music can tug at your heart strings,

Music can remind you of the beautiful things,

Music can offer you hope,

Music can help you cope,

Music can get you through times that are tough,

Times that are a little rough,

Music can cheer you up,

Music can put a smile back on your face,

Music can take you to that happy place,

Music can make you smile,

Music can get you through the ironing pile,

Music can start you crying,

Music can encourage you to keep on trying,

There is music for every feeling,

Music can do a lot of healing,

Music can encourage you to do some soul

searching,

Yes music,

Every lyric,

Seems to do that trick,

And get you to think,

That's music.

A Million Love Poems

No. 1

The first poem in this book for the Princess inspired by songs that remind me of her is "A Million Love Poems". This poem was inspired by the Gary Barlow/Take That song – A Million Love Songs. I'm not a song writer but given how much the Princess inspires me, I reckon I could easily write a million poems about her, the words, the inspiration just flows easily. I thought this would be an appropriate one to open the book with.

I am someone by nature that struggles with talking feelings and emotions tending to instead bottle them up and find it especially hard telling someone that I really care/love them. I don't know whether it is a fear thing, fear of looking stupid, fear of being rejected, fear of being hurt, perhaps a combination of all three and maybe a bit of cowardice in there too or maybe all cowardice and if I say it's because I'm scared of rejection and looking stupid enough times I may actually believe it myself. I do wish I could just tell the Princess the truth how I feel and not feel scared of rejection when she said no but I can't. So instead of talking feelings and emotions I tend to write them down as a way of releasing how I feel and my feelings for the Princess come out in poem form, I hope they explain to her how I truly feel about her, I hope they show

her how beautiful, how sweet, how truly special
I think she is.

I'm not Gary Barlow,

Writing you a million love songs,

Poems instead,

Right from the heart, not the head,

That is my forte,

Princess, I hope they do say,

Princess, I hope you, they do show;

That to you, is where my heart belongs,

Princess, how I do struggle to reveal,

About you, how I really feel,

I'm a writer not a talker,

So I hope these poems tell ya,

That Princess with you I am so in love,

Believe me Princess, this isn't a bluff,

I think you're hot stuff!

So poem after poem,

Written especially for and dedicated to you,

The words just keep flowing,

Each poem written with love and the contents of

each … true!

I hope you, they do show,

That you are the most beautiful, most special,

most sweetest girl I know!

Circumstance

No. 2

The second poem in this book for the Princess inspired by songs that remind me of her is inspired by George Michael's "A Different Corner".

This song really hits home with me and the line "Turn a different corner and we never would have met" really rings true because had a certain circumstance in my life been different, I.e. had I not left my previous job for pastures new, I never would have met the Princess as the Princess replaced me and as I only moved two minutes down the road I still pop in the old workplace of a lunchtime for a chat with my old colleagues and the Princess now as we have become friends though I do harbour secret feelings for her.

Princess, maybe it was meant,

Maybe it was fate that I went,

Maybe it was a gift that was heaven sent,

For me,

To meet thee,

Who knew you'd bring me so much glee?

Princess, who knew,

That when I left for pastures new,

That a couple of months later I'd meet you,

8th February to be precise,

A day so nice,

A day so happy - upon that you cannot put a

price,

It all could have been a different story,

For you and me,

Had I not gone,

I would never have met you – the special one!

So, Princess maybe it was more fate than chance,

Because it all could have been different had there

been a different circumstance.

Read How I Feel

No. 3

The third poem in this book for the Princess inspired by songs that remind me of her is inspired by Emeli Sande's "Read All About It".

Princess, I'm hopeless at talking feelings and emotions, I struggle to find the right words to say, I desperately want you to know how I really feel about you but I'm scared Princess, scared of making a fool of myself, scared I guess of being rejected, laughed at, embarrassed, heartbroken besides which I would probably sound a right fool trying to find the right words to tell you how I really feel so I've done what I always do and release my feelings in writing and written you a book of poems (another one!) Hope you can see what you really mean to me when you read these, I hope they show you how I really feel.

Emeli Sande's song "Read All About It" inspired this poem, as I said I'm hopeless at talking feelings and emotions so I've written them down in poems for you Princess so please read how I feel about you.

Princess, I've written a book for you,

An anthology,

Of Poetry,

What's inside,

Describe my feelings for you that I hide,

The contents of the book are true,

A book especially for you,

From me,

To thee,

I hope when you read this you will see,

What you truly mean to me,

I hope these poems do reveal,

Exactly how I feel,

These are from my heart,

For the girl whom from the very start,

From when we first met,

I knew on her, my heart was set,

The girl I think about day and night,

The girl for whom I fell in love with at first sight,

I thought it would be romantic,

Perhaps a tactic,

A way,

A way to finally say,

Princess, I'm crazy about you,

It's true,

I thought instead of chocolates and flowers,

I'd put in the hours,

Put in the time,

Do something original,

Something to show my love is unconditional,

Something Princess you can say is all mine,

And do something different,

And write you a book of poems,

Hope they say what they are meant,

I hope you like them, the words just seemed to

keep flowing,

So, Princess I hope they show,

How crazy I am about you,

I hope they show that for you there is nothing I

wouldn't do,

Princess, I wrote a book especially for you.

Princess – This Is Your Poem

No. 4

The fourth poem in this book for the Princess inspired by songs that remind me of her is inspired by Elton John's "Your Song".

Well Princess, instead of a song it's a poem and it's for you! Inspired by you and dedicated to and especially for you ... not just this poem but a whole book of them! Hopefully you'll see from reading them just how amazing, how beautiful, how sweet, how lovely, how special I think you are!

This is a poem especially for you Princess,

For whom my feelings I cannot express,

You look like an Angel,

Over my heart you have a strangle,

With your long dark hair,

That's silky and smooth,

I wish I had the confidence to make a move,

Do I dare?

For you my heart cries,

Looking into your beautiful brown eyes,

I can see your soul,

In my heart there's a hole,

It's where you should be,

Come on Princess, complete me!

Your sweet smile lights up the room,

When I see you my heart just goes boom, boom,

You're funny and clever,

For a Princess like you, I'll wait forever!

You move with elegance and grace,

A real lady,

I wish you was my baby,

I could never tire of seeing your beautiful face,

You're gentle and kind,

You're forever on my mind,

You're whom I always think about,

I love you, I want to shout,

You, Princess, are a dear friend,

If I tell you how I feel,

It could all end,

Would I ever heal?

Do I risk it all?

It's a tough call!

So Princess, here's a poem,

That I am hoping,

Does reveal,

How I really feel,

And tells you that I am so in love with you,

And for you there is nothing I wouldn't do.

I Couldn't Help Falling In Love With You

No. 5

The fifth poem in this book for the Princess inspired by songs that remind me of her is inspired by Elvis Presley's "Can't Help Falling In Love", though I also love the UB40 version too.

This song inspired this poem because as I said it may sound cliché, it may sound cheesy but it's true. I remember the first day I met the Princess for the first time – 8th February 2016 – I'll never ever forget it – I came away from meeting her for the first time and as I was walking back to my office I couldn't get her out of my head, I remember muttering to myself, my exact words were "Oh God, she is stunning, she is absolutely gorgeous". For me it was definitely love at first sight, I knew this because of feelings I had never felt before with any other girl at all, the racing heart, pounding, skipping a beat, the butterflies feeling in my stomach, feelings I thought were just a myth made up by Hollywood or authors to sell movies and books but they're not made up, they're real feelings and because of the Princess I now know this because I felt them the first time I saw her and every time I see her now and since our first meeting.

I couldn't help falling in love with you,

There was nothing to stop it that I could do,

I remember coming away from our very first meeting,

My heart was pounding and beating,

Butterflies in my stomach were stirring,

Strange feelings I'd never ever felt before were occurring,

Feelings I thought that didn't really exist,

Feelings at first I dismissed,

Putting them down to some other explanation,

My heart argued without hesitation,

Whispering "she's the one",

"I'm in it for the long run",

Princess, Upon you my heart is set,

Has been since the day we met,

That day is the best yet,

It may sound cliché,

But straightaway,

I fell for you instantly,

Me in love with thee,

Princess, I couldn't help falling in love with you,

There was nothing to stop it that I could do,

Princess, it's true,

I'm so in love with you,

Now, always and forever,

Princess forget that never.

Cupid

No. 6

The sixth poem in this book for the Princess inspired by songs that remind me of her is a poem from my first book "Poems For A Princess" but I feel this poem goes well with the Sam Cooke song also entitled "Cupid".

I do hope that Cupid's arrow lands me the Princess and I get the happy fairytale ending that I dream of with the Princess, you know my happily ever after.

Come on cupid,

Don't be stupid!

Get out your bow,

And fire your arrow!

So please take aim,

In this love game,

Your target for me ...

Is she;

The Princess;

Whom I like best,

She's better than all the rest!

33

I believe she's my fate,

So cupid don't wait,

Don't hesitate,

Fire, GO!

Don't miss though!

Let your arrow hit,

And to her I will forever commit,

She's the girl I adore,

And love her forevermore ...

Will I,

Until the day I die.

Words

No. 7

The seventh poem in this book for the Princess inspired by songs that remind me of her is also a poem from my first book "Poems For A Princess" but I feel this poem goes well with the Bee Gees song also entitled "Words".

As I touched on previously, I am hopeless when it comes to expressing my feelings and emotions verbally and therefore tend to express them by writing them down. This is what I hope this book also does – tells the Princess again how I really feel about her. Like the song suggests, I know these are only words in poem form but Princess, they are all I have to try and win your heart, to show you, to tell you how I feel about you. Princess, you should know I'm serious if this is the second book I've written for you. Princess they're only words but they're all true, what I write, I feel and I just want to let you know how special I think you are.

Words, so many from which to choose,

So how is it so I can never find the right words to

use?

To tell the Princess,

That I love best,

How I feel,

My feelings I want to reveal,

This isn't good for a supposed wordsmith!

Perhaps me being good with words is a myth?

They have to be perfect,

I cannot afford any defect,

They have to have meaning,

They have to be words said with feeling,

They have to be words of passion and love,

To show her that she is the girl I have always

dreamed of,

They have to be words oh so true,

They have to say to her that I love you.

Words, so many from which to choose,

Difficult to know which to use.

Love Poems

No. 8

The eighth poem in this book for the Princess inspired by songs that remind me of her is inspired by Elvis Presley's "Love Letters".

This song inspired this poem because when listening to the lyrics whilst ironing one Sunday morning, the line "Love Letters Straight From The Heart" got me thinking about all the poems I have written for the Princess and my poems come straight from the heart, they're real, they are based on real feelings, my real feelings and they basically say everything I wish I had the courage to tell her face to face but can't, be that whether it's being afraid of looking/sounding stupid, fear of rejection, not wanting to upset or embarrass or make the Princess feel awkward so I just hope that when reading this, the Princess sees how I really feel about her.

Love poem after love poem,

The words just continue flowing,

Princess, you are my inspiration,

These poems to you, a dedication,

Poems straight from this heart of mine,

Each line,

Beautiful,

Deep and meaningful,

Truthful,

And thoughtful,

These love poems are just my way,

To say,

From me,

To thee,

Princess, it's true,

I'm so in love with you.

No Could She Be Prince

No. 9

The ninth poem in this book for the Princess inspired by songs that remind me of her is inspired by Prince's "The Most Beautiful Girl In The World".

This song was an easy pick to inspire a poem. The title alone reminds me of the Princess. In my bias opinion the Princess is the most beautiful girl in the world. Prince, in the song, posed the question "Could you be the most beautiful girl in the world", well if you ask me there is no "Could she be ..." - she IS the most beautiful girl in the world.

This actually came about one night when I was lying in bed awake one night unable to sleep and this song came on the radio and it instantly got me thinking about the Princess.

This song also plays a strange role in my life in a "Groundhog Day" sort of way, well this song and the Stevie Wonder song "Isn't she Lovely", which inspired the next poem in the book. There is something strange that happens, some force at work if you like, because it doesn't matter what time I climb into bed, the first song that plays when I do is one of the above songs and then strangely, whatever time I seem to wake up, again its either one of the songs above that plays on the radio.

Prince posed the question,

I can answer it no hesitation!

Could you be ...

It's a definite yes,

Princess,

From me,

Ask me something harder that was too easy!

You are the most beautiful girl in the world,

From me to you compliments are always hurled,

No could you be ...

If you ask me,

You are the most beautiful,

And that IS indisputable!

Princess, with you I've fallen in love,

So beautiful it's as if you were sent from above,

So Prince, there's no "could she be",

The most beautiful girl in the world IS she!

So Princess, let me be your Prince,

In love with you from the day we met and ever

since.

Stevie's Right

The tenth poem in this book for the Princess inspired by songs that remind me of her is inspired by Stevie Wonder's "Isn't She Lovely". This poem also appeared in my first book entitled "Poems For A Princess" but I thought it was only apt that it went in this book also given that they are poems inspired by songs that remind me of the Princess and this song does just that.

Again, this came about one night when I was lying in bed awake one night unable to sleep and this song came on the radio and it instantly got me thinking about the Princess just like the Prince song that inspired the poem before this one.

As I mentioned in the poem before this one, this song plays a strange role in my life in a "Groundhog Day" sort of way, this song and as mentioned previously, the Prince song, "The Most Beautiful Girl In The World", there is something strange that happens, some force at work if you like, because it doesn't matter what time I climb into bed, the first song that plays when I do is one of the above songs and then strangely, whatever time I seem to wake up, again its either one of the songs above that plays on the radio.

The words made this song an obvious choice to inspire a poem because like the song asks, "Isn't she lovely, isn't she wonderful, truly the Angel's best", yes, yes and yes to all of those, the Princess, is definitely all three in my bias opinion.

The Princess, is the most beautiful, most loveliest, most sweetest girl that I know, if only she knew how I really feel, if only she knew my real feelings that I harbour for her.

Stevie Wonder's right,

What a man of foresight!

It's almost as if you, he knew,

It's as if the song lyrics were written especially for

you!

I think so anyway,

Here's what I have to say,

Listen Princess,

The lyrics describe you best!

Stevie sang "Isn't she lovely"

Princess, yes you are!

He'll have no arguments from me!

You are the most beautiful girl in the world –

no-one is on a par,

Stevie sang "Isn't she wonderful"

Princess, yes you are - you make my life colourful!

Stevie sang "Isn't she Precious"

Yes Princess, you are,

I admire you from afar,

You're luscious,

You leave me breathless,

You're gorgeous,

Princess,

I'm obsessed!

Stevie sang "Isn't she pretty"

Princess, yes you are - please let me Love you ...

Oh please permit me,

For you there isn't anything I wouldn't do!

Stevie sang "Truly the Angel's best"

Yes Princess, you are! - Better than all the rest!

There is no contest!

So I conclude that Stevie you are a man of
foresight,
About the Princess you are right,
For she is truly lovely, wonderful, precious, pretty
and the best!
To know her I am truly blessed,
Being her man is my quest,
But to achieve it, it's time I confessed,
For long enough I've kept my feelings
suppressed,
It's about time they were expressed.

The First Time I Saw You

No. 11

The eleventh poem in this book for the Princess inspired by songs that remind me of her is inspired by Roberta Flack's "The First Time I Ever Saw Your Face".

When I first heard this song, it reminded me of the Princess and the first time I ever saw her. I remember the meeting well, I remember every moment spent in her company, I cherish every second spent in her company.

I remember our first meeting, I walked in the office, it was her first day replacing me at my old workplace, we were introduced and I remember the first thing I noticed about her was her beautiful brown eyes and her cute, sexy smile. We had a chat, I asked how she was finding her first day etc. etc. as well as giving her a few "office survival tips". It was strange how my heart was instantly captured by her, my heart was racing, pounding, beating my chest, I had a strange feeling in my stomach (I thought it was indigestion) it wasn't it was butterflies, it was only when I came away from our first meeting and was walking back to my workplace (only 2 minutes away!) that these feelings I was experiencing was pointing to falling in love. Previously, I had always dismissed their existence, calling them a myth, butterflies, racing heart, just made up by Hollywood and writers to sell films and books but no, they are actually real feelings and this I now knew because I was feeling them! I remember as I was walking I muttered to myself "Oh God, she's so beautiful, stunning, gorgeous" you probably guessed I was instantly smitten! My heart was set upon the Princess, my heart whispered she is the one!

Yes, never ever will I forget the moment I first met the Princess.

Never will I ever forget,

The very first time you and I met,

8th February,

A memorable day for me,

Meeting you for the very first time,

I had no idea what affect you'd have on this heart

of mine,

When I walked in, we were introduced

I left with my heart seduced,

By you,

Who knew?

Who'd a thought it?

Cupid's arrow had hit!

Something I couldn't have predicted,

Something I never expected!

I remember entering,

And sitting there was this beautiful little thing,

Oh, almost instantly,

I could feel you doing something to me,

My heart began to sing,

Never before had I experienced this kind of
thing!

We had a little chat,

About how your first day was going and that,

I'll tell you no lies,

The first thing I noticed about you was your
beautiful brown eyes,

And your cute, sexy smile,

Meanwhile,

Immediately,

Instantly,

My heart was melted,

I knew that this memory was never going to be
deleted,

But forever cherished,

To me my heart said,

She's the one,

The most beautiful girl bar none,

She is who I choose,

My heart, how could I refuse!

Oh, how my heart did race,

As soon as I saw your face,

My heartbeat was all over the place,

Oh, how fast my heart was beating,

Following our first meeting,

How funny,

Was the feeling of butterflies in my tummy,

How strange when I left,

I felt bereft,

Thinking, feeling like this already?

Whoa, heart be steady,

My heart replied "I'm in love"

The stark realisation of truth,

Strewth!

Good heavens above,

It's true,

Princess, I'm in love with you!

It may sound cliché,

But me,

I fell in love with you at first glance,

Princess, what I'd give for a chance,

A romance,

Princess, never will I forget,

That special day that you and I first met.

My Heart Skips A Beat

No. 12

The twelfth poem in this book for the Princess inspired by songs that remind me of her is inspired by Olly Murs' "Heart Skips a Beat".

The song title made this song an easy choice, an easy choice because it is what happens to me every time I see the Princess. Every time, I see her, my heart races, pounds my chest and skips beats, it's a wonder the Princess cannot hear it. The heart skipping a beat, I thought was just a myth, made up to sell romance in books and films but now because of the Princess, I now know that it really does exist, never experiencing it before indicates that I had never met anyone as special as the Princess before to make me experience this feeling so it just shows how special she is.

It's strange,

How every time we meet,

You always cause a change,

In my heartbeat,

Ever since we first met,

Upon you my heart has been set,

As soon as I walk in the room,

And as soon as I see you,

It's true,

My heart just goes boom, boom,

How my heart does race,

The rhythm all over the place,

Oh Princess, how my heart does skip a beat,

Every time we meet.

Gorgeous

No. 13

The thirteenth poem in this book for the Princess inspired by songs that remind me of her is inspired by Baby Bird's "You're Gorgeous".

A short and sweet poem summed up in one simple word – "Gorgeous" because Princess – You are!

Gorgeous,

One of many words I could use to describe you,

Princess,

I don't need a thesaurus,

When one simple word will do,

Gorgeous,

Says it all, nothing more, nothing less.

Perfect The Way You Are

No. 14

The fourteenth poem in this book for the Princess inspired by songs that remind me of her is inspired by Bruno Mars' "Just The Way You Are".

One night listening to the radio and this song came on, it instantly got me thinking about the Princess. It got me thinking how I think she is perfect, she is the girl I worship and idolise (if only she knew, huh!).

The Princess is the most beautiful girl in the world, she is sweet and lovely, funny and bubbly, she's smart and she's clever, the most beautiful girl ever. She is … Perfect!

The Princess is so sweet and modest that I think she doesn't know just how beautiful and how perfect she is but Princess, take it from me, you are so, so beautiful, in my biased eyes you are perfect.

As I look on from afar,

Admiring you,

What I know is true,

You are perfect the way you are,

Your beautiful dark hair,

Your stunning looks,

I can't help but stand and stare,

You're perfect in my books,

Princess you are beautiful,

It's indisputable,

To you no-one comes close,

To me you're like a drug,

Addicted,

Seeing you gives me a dose,

Falling in love with you I should have predicted,

I do indeed have the love bug!

Your smile so warm and friendly,

Perfection is what I see,

Princess, you're so lovely,

Princess, you are perfect to me,

So never change Princess,

You're the best,

You're perfect just the way you are.

You're So Beautiful

No. 15

The fifteenth poem in this book for the Princess inspired by songs that remind me of her is inspired by Joe Cocker's "You Are So Beautiful (to me)".

Princess – the title says it all really, you are so, so beautiful Princess, I don't think you know just how beautiful you are! I hope this second book of poems for you reiterates just how beautiful and how special I think you are.

Beautiful,

That's what you are,

Its indisputable,

No other girl is on a par!

Beautiful,

That's you!

Its indisputable,

It's true.

Beautiful,

With your lovely dark hair, smooth and silky,

Whether straight or wavy,

You always look lovely,

Beautiful,

Its indisputable,

Beautiful,

I'll tell you no lies,

I love your beautiful brown eyes,

You're the girl that my eyes do idolise,

I hope your eyes are ones which never cries,

I could lose myself in your beautiful eyes oh so
brown,

Staring lovingly into them I'd happily drown,

Beautiful,

Its indisputable.

Beautiful,

With your cute, sexy smile,

For you is what makes living worthwhile,

For me

Because I'm so in love with thee,

For one of your smiles,

I'd walk a million miles,

Your smile is a beautiful gift,

Oh, how seeing one gives me a lift,

Beautiful,

Its indisputable.

Beautiful,

Its indisputable,

You always look wonderful,

You always look phenomenal,

To quote Rod Stewart, you wear anything well,

I think you're beautiful – can you tell?

You're a lady who is elegant,

You must be heaven sent,

Princess, you're beautiful,

Its indisputable,

Beautiful,

That's what you are,

Its indisputable,

I'm in love with you from afar.

Beautiful,

That's you!

Its indisputable,

It's true.

My Eyes Adore You

No. 16

The sixteenth poem in this book for the Princess inspired by songs that remind me of her is inspired by Frankie Valli's "My Eyes Adored You".

Princess, you know I find it hard to believe that you haven't ever noticed me/caught me staring at you, admiring you, gazing at you adoringly and lovingly, like a puppy dog even.

Princess, the very first moment my eyes met yours and I saw your beautiful brown eyes, your smile, I knew you were something/someone special by what was happening to me, you set my heart racing, my temperature rising, I'm sure I went as red as a traffic light! You started that weird sensation in my tummy or butterflies as I now know them as, yes Princess my eyes worship, idolise and adore you!

Look into my eyes,

They will tell you no lies,

Princess, here's the score,

You are the girl that my eyes do adore,

My eyes,

You they idolise,

Princess, my eyes,

They will tell you no lies,

You're the girl I adore,

You're the girl I'd do anything for.

My Eyes Only See …

The seventeenth poem in this book for the Princess inspired by songs that remind me of her is inspired by The Bee Gees "I Can't See Nobody".

This song actually come to my attention whilst ironing one Sunday morning (I can't iron unless I have a CD on) I find it tedious otherwise! Anyway, as I was saying, I was listening to the Bee Gees whilst ironing and this track came on and one line really stood out and grabbed my attention and inspired this poem. The line "I can't see nobody, no I can't see nobody, my eyes can only look at you" – Princess, this line got me thinking about you, ever since you and I met, no other girl has gotten my attention like you command my attention, my heart doesn't even flutter when I see another girl who would be perceived as attractive, my heart only ever races and I only ever get butterflies when I see or think about you. My eyes, obviously don't notice anyone but you. Princess you are indeed special, truly special.

My eyes, they do not notice,

Anybody else but you,

It's true,

Princess,

You're the only choice,

The only girl my eyes notice,

My Princess,

My little Miss,

My little Miss Sunshine,

The girl I wish was mine,

The girl I think about all the time,

My eyes only see you,

My eyes only see the girl for whom there's
nothing I wouldn't do,

My eyes only see the little dark haired cutie,

My eyes only see your radiant beauty,

My eyes only see your beautiful brown eyes that I
could get lost in,

My eyes only see the girl whose heart I want to
win,

My eyes only see your beautiful, cute, sexy smile,

My eyes only see the girl who defines beauty and
style,

My eyes only see the girl who makes waking up
every day worthwhile,

My eyes only see the girl who is sweet and lovely,

My eyes only see the girl who is funny and
bubbly,

My eyes only see the girl who's awoken feelings I
never knew existed in me,

My eyes only see thee,

Princess, my eyes, they only notice,

YOU! Princess,

Unforgettable Is The Girl …

No. 18

The eighteenth poem in this book for the Princess inspired by songs that remind me of her is inspired by Nat King Cole's "Unforgettable"

This song is so apt, such an apt title – Unforgettable, and the Princess certainly is that. My heart cannot forget the Princess, my heart has chosen her and did the day that I first met her. I kinda knew then that she was something else, something special, the way she made me felt, felt like I'd never felt before, butterflies in my tummy, my heart racing and pounding and all because of this special girl that I had only just met.

I remember everything about the Princess that she tells me, from her favourite doughnut to strange anniversaries she has such as when she passed her driving test – I remember everything she says because I care and I'm interested, I could listen to her for hours, she could read the phonebook and I wouldn't be bored or lose attention. I struggle to tear myself away when I have to leave I love her company that much! I cherish every single second spent with her in her company I remember every moment and cherish it.

I'd love to spend forever with her making memories together.

The Princess truly is special and unforgettable.

Unforgettable,

Unforgettable is the girl who is adorable,

Unforgettable is the girl who is beautiful,

Unforgettable is the girl with the beautiful brown eyes,

Unforgettable is the girl that I idolise,

Unforgettable is the girl with the sexy, cute smile,

Unforgettable is the girl who makes waking up every day worthwhile,

Unforgettable is the girl who oozes class and style,

Unforgettable is the girl with the silky smooth dark hair,

Unforgettable is the girl at whom I can't help but stand and stare,

Unforgettable is the girl I think about all the time,

Unforgettable is the girl I wish I could call mine,

Unforgettable is the girl who is sweet and lovely,

Unforgettable is the girl who is funny and bubbly,

Unforgettable is the girl that makes my heart race,

Unforgettable is the girl with the most beautiful
face,

Unforgettable is the girl who defines elegance,

Unforgettable is the girl for whom I'd give
anything for a chance,

Unforgettable is the girl whom I'd love to
romance,

Unforgettable is the girl who gives me butterflies,

Unforgettable is the girl for whom my heart cries,

Unforgettable is the girl I adore,

Unforgettable is the girl for whom I'd do
anything for,

Unforgettable is you!

My Heart Has Chosen You!

No. 19

The nineteenth poem in this book for the Princess inspired by songs that remind me of her is inspired by John Travolta's and Olivia Newton John's – "You're the one that I want" (the Grease soundtrack)

This song was a pretty easy choice really, I remember the day I first met the Princess (I'll never forget it) but it was when I left that first meeting and was walking back to my office that I realised I was thinking about her still, I recall muttering to myself how beautiful she was and my heart was pounding and racing, I had a strange feeling in my tummy (butterflies) and I remember my heart whispering "she's the one, she's the one I want" and how can you argue with what your heart wants and what's inside it? The Princess and infinite amounts of love are in mine for her.

Two thousand and sixteen,

To be precise, 8th February,

A day that will forever live in my memory,

Let me explain what I mean!

For that day,

With me will forever stay,

Remembered for a meeting,

Which when over, left my heart beating,

Pounding like a drum,

Something special had begun,

Feelings I'd never felt before,

What was it?

At first, I wasn't sure,

Then suddenly it hit,

Like a smack to the face,

It all fell into place,

The racing heart and the butterflies,

It was easy to surmise,

I didn't need no answer from above,

With you I was IN LOVE!

You! Chosen by my heart,

From the very start,

My heart whispered she's the one,

My heart – you've won,

My heart says you're the special one!

Never Met A Girl Like You Before

No. 20

The twentieth poem in this book for the Princess inspired by songs that remind me of her is inspired by Edwyn Collins – " Never Met A Girl Like You Before"

The song title is so apt, so true, never before had I ever met a girl like the Princess before, a girl so beautiful, so sweet, so lovely, so special.

I didn't know what love was, proper love until I met the Princess as never before had I ever experienced the racing, pounding heart, the butterflies in my stomach, the getting tongue tied, the not being able to get her out of my mind – nope, before meeting the Princess, I had never met a girl like her before, a girl so special to make me feel what I feel, to get inside my heart, to make me fall in love, to capture my heart.

She truly is a special girl.

Princess, what I'm about to say,

Is true,

Until that day,

I had never met anyone like you,

Nope, never before,

Had I met someone whom I adore,

So much,

And as such,

Since you and I first met,

Upon you my heart has been set,

Princess, you are the girl,

That gives me a thrill,

Every time I see your face,

You make my heart race,

Princess, you give me butterflies,

Princess, you're for whom my heart cries,

Princess, it's true,

Until I met you,

I'd never felt these feelings,

Experiencing them, I now know their meanings!

That four letter word L – O – V – E

I'm in love with thee,

Princess, because of you, I smile more,

Princess, never ever have I met a girl like you before,

A girl so beautiful,

So special,

So sweet,

The loveliest girl I ever did meet,

A girl so lovely,

A girl who has taught me,

What it feels like to be in love,

She's an Angel – she must be sent from above!

Nope, I cannot recall,

Ever meeting a girl as special as you before!

Always On My Mind Is The Girl ...

No. 21

The twenty first poem in this book for the Princess inspired by songs that remind me of her is inspired by Elvis Presley's "Always On My Mind"

The song is an important song in my life as this song was played at my Mum's funeral – it was her favourite Elvis song so it already meant a lot to me for that reason and because of the Princess, it has taken on even more importance in my life.

This song is important and the song title so apt because as the title suggests "Always On My Mind", the Princess is always on my mind. I find that I think about her all the time, when I'm awake, every second seemingly, and when I'm asleep, I see her in my dreams, everything seemingly reminds me of her or starts me off thinking about her, well this song certainly does as it proves inspiring a poem as has the other songs mentioned in this book - inspiring poems and another book dedicated to and especially for her.

Yes, the truth is ever since I first met the Princess, she has always been on my mind since. My heart has chosen her, I am, I am in love with her. I hope this book shows her/tells her.

Princess, ever since you and I first met,

I find,

That you girl, are always on my mind,

Upon you my heart is well and truly set,

You Princess, I cannot forget,

Day or night,

Dark or bright,

Asleep or awake,

My mind just doesn't take a break,

From thoughts of you,

You're in everything I do,

When I'm happy,

It's because of thee,

When I'm sad,

Think of you,

I no longer feel blue,

But instead glad,

Think of you and I smile,

Think of you and it shows me life is worthwhile,

Princess, whatever the circumstance,

I find,

That there's a good chance,

That you girl, are always on my mind.

The Beat Of My Heart Tells Me So

No. 22

The twenty second poem in this book for the Princess inspired by songs that remind me of her is inspired by Rod Stewart's "Every Beat Of My Heart"

Hearing this song one day got me thinking about the Princess again, it got me thinking how every time I see her my heart races and pounds or even the anticipation of seeing her, if I know I'm going to see her my heart will begin racing and pounding my chest.

Yes indeed, every beat of my heart does tell me that I am so in love with her. My heart doesn't behave like this when I see any other girl. Princess you are truly special and Princess, it looks as if my heart has chosen you. My heart beats for you Princess, for you.

I don't have to be smart,

I don't have to be Einstein,

To know that every beat of this heart,

Of mine,

Tells me that with you,

I'm so in love, it's true,

The beat of my heart does tell me so,

Thump, thump it does go,

For you girl,

Are the one that gives my heart a thrill,

Whenever I see your face,

How my heart rate does quicken pace,

Whenever I have you on my mind,

I find,

My heart beats quicker and quicker,

My heart tells me I'm in love with her,

Good heavens above,

I'm in love!

Every beat of my heart tells me so,

Oh Princess, I wish you did know!

The Way You Make Me Feel
(Version 1)

No. 23

The twenty third poem in this book for the Princess inspired by songs that remind me of her is inspired by Michael Jackson's "The Way You Make Me Feel".

I chose this song because until I met the Princess, I just thought all the "symptoms" if you will, of being in love, the racing heart, the butterflies in the stomach, getting tongue tied, the puppy dog eyes, were all made up by Hollywood to sell romantic films or by authors to sell romantic books and the notion of love. However, I know for myself that those "symptoms, those feelings" they're not myths, they're not made up, they're very much real, real because that's how I feel, I experience them whenever I see the Princess, no-one else makes me feel like or experience them only the Princess. That's how I know for the first time, I am in love.

I never thought I would feel like this, and I have tried to turn these feelings off but I can't, I just can't and I have tried oh so very hard, it's impossible when your heart has chosen someone.

The way you make me feel,

Princess, it's unreal,

Its surreal,

You've made me feel like I've never felt before,

What it was,

At first I wasn't sure,

But of my heart, you're the boss!

Never before had I experienced the heart race,

The rhythm all over the place,

Never before had I experienced the butterflies,

Never before had a girl ever brought tears to my

eyes,

Princess, I love you with all my heart,

Yet my heart and eyes,

Cries,

Because we're apart,

Princess, you I adore,

I can't help but stand and stare in awe,

Princess, in your presence I get tongue tied,

It's as if I'm petrified,

Of saying something stupid or looking like a fool,

Princess, in your presence it's hard for me to keep
calm and cool,

I try to speak but often stutter,

Simple sentences I cannot mutter,

You probably think what's wrong with this nutter!

But Princess,

I confess,

Me,

You make me happy,

I love spending time in your company,

I cherish every second,

I never want it to end,

The dream for me?

It's easy,

To spend forever,

Together,

With thee,

Good Lord above,

I'm in love,

Princess, the way you make me feel,

It's surreal!

The Way You Make Me Feel
(Version 2)

No. 24

The twenty fourth poem in this book for the Princess inspired by songs that remind me of her is another version of the poem "The Way You Make Me Feel" inspired by the Michael Jackson song of the same title. I don't usually write two versions of poems but I couldn't choose between the two so I have decided to put both versions in. You, the readers will no doubt be able to decide which version you prefer or hopefully like both!

Again, this poem just describes how the Princess makes me feel. The racing heart, the butterflies, jelly legs, puppy dog eyes etc.

Princess,

You I've got to address,

I have something to say,

And this is my way,

A poem for you,

I hope what I try and say gets through,

Princess,

I was blessed,

The day we met,

And ever since upon you my heart has been set,

For me it was love at first sight,

And ever since that first meeting,

I realise you're the reason my heart keeps on

beating,

I can't help but think of you day and night,

I've never felt like this before,

Princess, this is the score;

I'm addicted,

It's something I couldn't have predicted,

Falling for you,

My heart to you will be forever true,

You're like a drug,

I've got the love bug,

Like a magnet,

To you I was instantly attracted,

Princess, you I idolise,

Whenever I see you I get butterflies,

In my belly,

My legs turn to jelly,

Like a drug, seeing you gives me highs,

I thought it was all some kind of trick,

But it wasn't – I'm just love sick!

You're the reason I smile,

You're the reason for me that life is worthwhile,

Seeing you gives me a thrill,

You're a one in 7.4 billion girl, (7.4 billion people

on earth)

Princess, baby,

You amaze me,

At you I stand and look in awe,

Princess, I've never felt like this before,

Princess, it's you I adore,

I'll love you forevermore,

So that's the score,

Princess, you've made me feel like I've never felt

before.

Dilemma

The twenty fifth poem in this book for the Princess inspired by songs that remind me of her is inspired by Nelly and Kelly's hit from a few years back also entitled "Dilemma".

This poem came about one Saturday night, I was flicking through the TV channels and this song came on one of the music channels and it instantly got me thinking about the Princess and the fact that I face a dilemma on whether I reveal to the Princess how I really feel about her.

I'm hoping at the time of writing this that the Princess will already have guessed my true feelings for her from my first book for her "Poems for a Princess" if not I hope this book definitely does it! If not then the next drastic step would be to get her a guide dog because I can't make it any more obvious than telling her myself – which I'm too scared to do – I guess it's the fear of looking stupid and the inevitable rejection perhaps. I keep telling myself that I haven't told her in person how I feel because I don't want to embarrass or make her feel awkward or risk losing her as a friend and I guess it's true but it's also because I'm a coward I guess.

Like the song title – it is a dilemma, if I tell her then there is a high chance of losing her as a friend and her hating me but I can't turn my feelings off, I've tried, believe me I've tried, I wish I could, I hate feeling this way, being powerless over my feelings and not being able to control my heart. My heart has chosen her, it loves her, it only ever races for her, no other girl even gets a flutter out of it, however, deep down, my head knows that she is way out of my league, and way too good for me, she's beautiful, sweet, lovely, funny, just special, my heart however won't listen, it loves her so much, it aches and pines for her. So there's my dilemma, listen to my heart or my head, either way my heart loses and will likely end up broken but "F" it I love her so I wrote another book for her – I'll wait forever for her in the hope that one day I get my happily ever after with her, my fairytale ending.

Like Nelly,

And Like Kelly,

I have a dilemma,

Do I tell her?

Express,

To the Princess,

How I truly feel?

Do I dare reveal?

Like Nelly,

And like Kelly,

I have a dilemma,

Do I tell her?

Do I tell the Princess the funny feeling I get in

my belly?

Whenever I see the Princess my stomach ends up

in knots,

She's the girl for whom I have the hots!

Like Nelly,

And like Kelly,

I have a dilemma,

Do I tell her?

Do I tell the Princess how when I see her my

heart skips a beat?

Do I tell her how she knocks me off my feet?

Like Nelly,

And like Kelly,

I have a dilemma,

Do I tell her?

Do I tell the Princess that the day we first met;

Is my greatest yet?

Do I dare tell her that ever since on her my heart

has been set?

Like Nelly,

And like Kelly,

I have a dilemma,

Do I tell her?

Do I tell the Princess that I can't help but think

of her day and night?

Do I dare tell the Princess that with her, I fell in

love at first sight?

Like Nelly,

And like Kelly,

I have a dilemma,

Do I tell her?

Do I tell the Princess that her I do adore?

She's the girl I would do anything for!

Like Nelly,

And like Kelly,

I have a dilemma,

Do I tell her?

Do I tell the Princess what she truly means to

me?

Do I tell her that her man is what I yearn to be?

I wish she could make it easy,

And just see,

Like Nelly,

And like Kelly,

I have a dilemma,

Do I tell her?

Do I tell the Princess that she's the girl that can

make my dreams come true?

Do I finally be honest and say to her, "Princess, I love you!".

Like Nelly,

And like Kelly,

I have a dilemma,

Do I tell her?

Do I finally reveal to her the feelings that I hide?

Do I finally tell her of the love I harbour for her inside?

Like Nelly,

And like Kelly,

I have a dilemma,

Do I tell her?

Do I tell the Princess that to me she's the very best?

That she's better than all the rest!

Like Nelly,

And like Kelly,

I have a dilemma,

Do I tell her?

To the Princess, is it time I confessed?

How I feel about the Princess?

Like Nelly,

And like Kelly,

I have a dilemma,

Do I tell her?

Do I tell the Princess that she's my number one?

Do I tell the Princess that she's the special one?

Like Nelly,

And like Kelly,

I have a dilemma,

Do I tell her?

Do I tell the Princess who is as beautiful as an

Angel that's sent from above;

That with her I'm in love!

Like Nelly,

And like Kelly,

I have a dilemma,

Do I tell her?

To the Princess, do I finally reveal;

About her, how I feel?

I know these feelings are real.

Like Nelly,

And like Kelly,

I have a dilemma,

Do I tell her?

Yes or no?

I just don't know!

Oh Princess, what do I do?

When I'm so madly in love with you!

Like Nelly,
And like Kelly,
I have a dilemma,
Do I tell her?

To quote Nelly,
And Kelly,
Princess, baby, I love you!
I do!

Like Nelly,
And like Kelly,
I have a dilemma,
Do I tell her?

I'll Love You For All Time

No. 26

The twenty sixth poem in this book for the Princess inspired by songs that remind me of her is inspired by Whitney Houston's "I will always love you".

They say you never forget your first love and that you'll always love them forever, well the Princess is my first love, first true, proper love – she's the only girl that has ever made my heart race and skip a beat like she does, the only girl that has ever given me that butterfly feeling in my tummy, the only girl who makes me smile as much as she does, the only girl that I can't forget, yep there's something special about the Princess.

Yep, the Princess is the girl I'm in love with and like the Whitney song, I will always love her and like my poem title, I'll love her for all time.

I'll love you for all time,

One day I hope to make you mine,

Where there is hope,

I just about cope,

Hope no matter how small,

I'll give it my all,

However impossible it may seem,

A guy can dream,

Of ending up together with his Princess,

All I can do is give it my best,

To try and beat the rest,

Just looking for a chance to prove to you,

For you there is nothing I wouldn't do,

Just seeking a chance,

A chance to show you some good old fashioned

romance,

I know inside what I feel,

Believe me it's real,

I fell in love with you at first sight,

I think about you day and night,

Yes, Princess,

I confess,

That I will love you from now until the end of

time,

Princess, I wish you were mine.

Waiting For The Special One!

No. 27

The twenty seventh poem in this book for the Princess inspired by songs that remind me of her is inspired by Foreigner's "Waiting for a girl like you".

Well actually I wrote this poem back in September 2016, and the story behind it is this:-

I was in the company of two friends on a Friday when my one friend, she asked "why am I single", "I'm a lovely guy", "I'm a nice man", "A sweet guy". I didn't answer, instead I stood there thinking, I'm waiting for a girl, a very special girl, the girl who has captured my heart, the Princess, no other girl interests me. I didn't just leave her there waiting for an answer, my other friend, she answered for me, she said "He's waiting for the special one", I smiled, because I was/am. It's funny but that friend who said that, at the time, she didn't know who the Princess was, but she has since guessed who the Princess is but promised me she wouldn't tell her.

I then heard the Foreigner song "Waiting for a girl like you" on the radio and thought this poem and song sort of go the song inspires a poem like this as it's true, I am waiting for a girl, a truly special girl, the Princess, the most beautiful, most sweetest, most loveliest girl I have ever met.

I will indeed wait for the Princess, forever if necessary, waiting for a happy ending, a happily ever after, a fairytale ending.

Why? Because she's truly special and has captured my heart. She's the girl my heart beats for, the girl that makes my heart race, the girl that gives me butterflies, the girl that I'm secretly and madly in love with.

It was Friday,

When a friend did say,

Why are you single?

You're a lovely guy!

Your Sweet!

A Nice Man!

Another friend did tell her;

He is waiting for the "Special One"

Not Mourinho – No!

The girl whom I worship the ground she walks

on!

It's true,

Yes Princess – I'm waiting for you!

For it's you for whom I really care,

You're the girl with whom I want to mingle,

You're the girl I've been in love with since the

moment we did meet,

Princess, I'm your number one fan,

And I want to be your man,

But Princess, to tell you how I feel,

I'm struggling to reveal,

Too shy,

To try,

Princess,

You're the best,

The number one,

Bar none,

Princess, you're the special one,

And I'm waiting for you,

To you I will be forever true,

For I love you!

I do,

For you I'll wait a lifetime,

To make you mine,

Princess, you're the one I'm waiting for,

Princess, you're the one I adore,

Yes, I'm waiting for the number one,

Bar none,

The Special one,

And Princess – it's you!

It Must Be Love – What Else Can It Be?

No. 28

The twenty eighth poem in this book for the Princess inspired by songs that remind me of her is inspired by Madness's "It Must Be Love".

This poem is inspired by the above mentioned song. It just seemed the apt choice to explain the feelings that the Princess gives me – I mean the feelings or symptoms if you will all point to me being diagnosed as being in love. The feelings I feel – I have never felt before – the racing heart whenever I think, write about or see the Princess – my heart never races whenever I see any other girl – so that tells me that the Princess is pretty damn special for that to happen. Also, the warm fuzzy feeling in my tummy, butterflies is how Hollywood and books describe it as – never feeling them before I put it down to indigestion – I guess I was always skeptical previously, I suppose because I had never felt these feelings before so I just doubted that they really existed instead saying the racing heart and butterflies were just made up to sell films by Hollywood and books to sell the notion of love, but now, thanks, to the Princess, I know that these feelings aren't made up, that they do exist, because for the first time ever I feel them, I experience them but only ever with the Princess.

Yep, it must indeed be love that I'm feeling.

Good heavens above,

I'm in love!

What else can it be?

These strange feelings taking over me?

Can only mean one thing,

The way that my heart does sing,

The way the heart does race,

The way it does quicken pace,

Whenever I see the Princess' beautiful face,

The way my heart just goes boom, boom,

The way she's constantly on my mind from the
rising of the sun,

To the descending of the moon,

Somethings begun!

The way my legs turn to jelly,

The funny feelings in my belly,

The feeling of butterflies,

The tears in my eyes,

When we're apart,

The way her name is seemingly whispered by my heart,

The way she is always on my mind,

The way she is my every thought,

And so, I try to find …,

Any excuse is sought…,

After,

To see her,

Just for a fix,

Of the girl who knocks me for six,

The girl with whom I'm in love,

The girl whom I constantly dream of,

The girl I adore,

The girl I'll do anything for,

For the girl I'd do anything,

To make her my everything,

Yes, the way I feel,

Surely does reveal,

That I am in L-O-V-E,

With thee,

It must be,

Surely,

That I'm in love,

Good heavens above,

It must be,

That I'm in love with thee!

What else could it be?

Princess, You Can Do Magic!

No. 29

The twenty ninth poem in this book for the Princess inspired by songs that remind me of her is inspired by Limmie and Family Cookin's "You can do magic".

This poem came about one night when I was watching an old re-run of a Top of the Pops episode and this song came on and as soon as I heard the "You can do magic", it instantly got me thinking about the Princess and how it's almost magical how just seeing her sends my heart racing and skipping beats, how seeing her stirs up a funny warm fuzzy feeling in my tummy (I think we established these as being butterflies), how she seemingly leaves me all hot and flustered and tongue tied, how she leaves me blushing as red as a traffic light, how she turns my legs to jelly, how she makes me smile constantly, how she is always on my mind and in every thought, how she has managed to get inside my heart – it's like magic!

It's not a trick,

It's magic,

Princess, baby,

See,

What you do to me,

I don't mind,

Because baby,

I love thee,

Princess, I'm under your spell,

For you I have fell,

You drew me in like a magnet,

To you I was instantly attracted,

I find you mesmerising,

Just a glimpse of you sends my temperature

rising,

My knees turn to jelly,

I get butterflies in my belly,

I get all flustered,

Words aren't easily mustered,

My heart does race,

As soon as I see your beautiful face,

My heart thumps my chest,

Boom, Boom,

It goes,

Seeing you lifts any doom and gloom,

In your presence I'm often froze,

My heart skips a beat,

You knock me off my feet,

Of you I'm in awe,

You're like a drug,

Seeing you leaves me wanting more,

This isn't a trick,

It's magic,

I have the love bug,

With you Princess,

I confess,

I'm in love with you,

And for you anything I will do,

It's not a trick,

It's magic,

The magic of love,

And this is how you make me feel,

These feelings for you are real.

My Heart Belongs To The Brown Eyed Girl

No. 30

The thirtieth poem in this book for the Princess inspired by songs that remind me of her is inspired by Van Morrison's "Brown Eyed Girl".

As mentioned previously, one of the first things I noticed when I first saw the Princess was her beautiful brown eyes, that and her smile. Looking into her beautiful eyes instantly melted my heart I guess, because when I came away from that first meeting, my heart was racing and butterflies were stirring in my tummy, I remember muttering to myself how beautiful she was.

I could happily get lost looking into her beautiful brown eyes, I sort of drown in them, it was lovely on one occasion, we sort of had a moment if that's the right word, the right description, we were chatting and for a moment, brief moment, only a matter of what 10 seconds or something but we just gazed into each other's eyes, it was like time had stood still, it was like we were the only two people in the room, we weren't but it was like that, it felt that way, it seemed like it lasted ages but it didn't, I don't know if anyone else noticed but I would imagine they would have, still it was a very special moment for me, something I'll always remember.

Yes, this song, whenever I hear it, always makes me think of the Princess and how she has captured my heart.

My heart belongs to the brown eyed girl,

The girl who gives me a thrill,

Whenever I see her,

Strange and peculiar,

Feelings take over,

Feelings I'd never experienced before,

What they were, I wasn't sure,

Not at the beginning,

But then whenever I saw her I realised I kept grinning,

My head was spinning,

Round and round,

With thoughts of her,

One after another,

My heart would pound and pound,

My heart would skip a beat,

She would knock me off my feet,

I had butterflies inside me,

I then realised that she,

Had me under her spell,

For her I had fell,

She is the girl I've fallen for,

She's the girl I adore,

Yes the girl with the brown eyes,

I idolise,

Chosen by my heart,

From the very start,

As soon as we first met,

Upon her my heart was set,

My heart belongs to her,

And will do forever,

Yes, the girl who gives me a thrill …,

The brown eyed girl.

She Does Something To Me

No. 31

The thirty first poem in this book for the Princess inspired by songs that remind me of her is inspired by Paul Weller's "You do something to me".

I heard this song one night whilst lying awake in bed and the line "you do something to me" got me thinking about the Princess and the way she makes me feel, so I knocked this poem up about how she stirs up the feelings or "symptoms" if you like of being in love in me whenever I see her, seeing her does something to me.

Yes she,

Does something to me,

Whenever she,

I do see,

For strange feelings taketh over me,

The heart,

Does start,

To race,

Quickening pace,

I go all red in the face,

I get all hot and flustered,

Words cannot be easily mustered,

My knees,

They freeze,

My legs turn to jelly,

Butterflies flutter in my belly,

Goodness sakes,

I get the shakes,

I get the puppy dog eyes as I gaze dreamily at her,

Daydreaming of me and her being together,

All this stuff,

Adds up to me being in love,

Yes, whenever her I see,

She,

Does something to me.

She's Gifted – She Makes Me Feel Lifted

No. 32

The thirty second poem in this book for the Princess inspired by songs that remind me of her is inspired by The Lighthouse Family and their hit "Lifted".

I heard this song on the radio one night and the song title hit me straight away "lifted", I instantly thought about the Princess and how she always makes me feel happy. I had noticed several times in the time I've known her that when I've felt sad, low, down, depressed etc., etc., there has always been one common factor that has always perked me up, that has always made me feel better, that has always "lifted" me, brightened my day, lifted my spirits etc., and that something ... that something is the Princess. She is a truly amazing girl. She's so special. If only she knew just how special.

Yes thinking about her or seeing her instantly makes me feel better, yep the Princess is better medicine than any doctor could prescribe!

The Princess is gifted,

Whenever I see her, I feel lifted,

She does know,

When I'm feeling low,

How to turn my frown,

Upside down,

She puts a smile back on my face again,

She makes me forget all the pain,

When I can't raise a smile,

She makes me feel worthwhile,

When I'm feeling sad,

She can make me glad,

When I'm out of sorts,

Just thoughts,

Of her,

Can make me feel better,

I know for sure,

That she is better than any cure,

That a doctor,

Could prescribe,

Because when I feel dead on the inside,

Thoughts of/or seeing her brings me back alive,

Yes, when I'm feeling blue,

She knows just what to do,

To lift my spirits,

When I'm in bits,

Me, she knows how to fix,

Me,

She knows how to make me happy,

Yes,

The Princess

She is gifted,

She always makes me feel lifted.

Princess Of My Heart

No. 33

The thirty third poem in this book for the Princess inspired by songs that remind me of her is inspired by Westlife's "Queen of my Heart".

I know the song is titled "Queen of my heart" but I refer to this special girl that the book is for as a "Princess" and she owns my heart, she's in my heart, she's who my heart has chosen, she makes my heart race, she makes my heart skip beats, she's the only girl that can do that to me, she's the only girl that makes me feel this way and so this poem was born.

You know, it sounds funny but when my heart thumps, It sort of sounds like it's saying her name when it beats, …, …, …

Yep, my heart belongs to her.

I've said earlier in the book that when I came away from that first meeting with the Princess, that my heart was racing, was pounding, I had the butterfly feeling in my tummy, I recall saying to myself how beautiful, how stunning, how gorgeous she was.

Yep, instantly she captured my heart. She's the Princess of my heart.

You're the Princess of my heart,

I knew from the very start,

Right from the outset,

From the very first moment we met,

That upon you my heart was set,

My heart chose you,

There was nothing I could do,

My heart whispered she's the one,

The special one,

Inside my heart is thee,

To my heart you have the key,

With my heart you are trusted,

I beg you, please don't leave it busted,

So Princess of my heart I ask thee,

Come with the key,

And let my love free,

For you are the Princess of my heart,

You have been right from the very start.

With You – Time Spent = Magic Moment

No. 34

The thirty fourth poem in this book for the Princess inspired by songs that remind me of her is inspired by Perry Como's "Magic Moments".

The song title alone easily explains how this song inspires me to write a poem for the Princess. Magic moments sums it up perfectly – every moment spent with the Princess is a magic moment, a highlight, a cherished time, special, something I'll always cherish and remember - every last second!!

Time unfortunately goes to quickly, to be honest spending all the time in the world with her wouldn't be enough, I'd still be greedy and want to spend even more time with her. I love every moment spent with the Princess, our little chats or just even seeing her and that beautiful smile of hers, I never forget anything she tells me, I hang on every word she says, she could read the phonebook and I'd remember everything she said.

Yep, when the time comes to say goodbye to this world and the Angels say "hey Mark, what did you love about life most?" I will say, "easy, the Princess and every second spent with her!".

Yes, so there it is, every moment spent with the Princess is a moment I'll treasure and cherish forever, every moment indeed is a magic moment.

I wish you knew,

That every moment spent with you,

Is a moment I will treasure,

Forever,

Every moment, I'll forget never,

With you every moment spent,

Is like its heaven sent,

From above,

Every second with you, I love,

Every second spent with you is a precious gift,

Spending time with you gives me a lift,

Time spent with you is always worthwhile,

Time spent with you always makes me smile,

I must say,

Spending time with you is my highlight of the day,

For me,

Every moment spent with thee,

Is a beautiful everlasting memory,

For all eternity,

Time with you goes too quickly,

If you ask me,

Every second spent with you I cherish,

To spend forever with you is my only wish,

Time spent with you is my happiest,

Time spent with you Princess,

Is the best,

I wish time spent together,

Lasted longer,

And when the Angels ask me what time of life I liked best,

I'll say time spent with the Princess,

With you any time spent,

For me is a magic moment.

Santa All I Want For Christmas Is …

No. 35

The thirty fifth poem in this book for the Princess inspired by songs that remind me of her is inspired by Mariah Carey's "All I Want For Christmas".

I know it's early and at the time of writing, Christmas is 5 months away but I thought I'd get in early with my list for Santa, you'll see I'm not one for asking for loads, in fact only one gift I would like and that is the most beautiful, sweetest and most special gift of all … the Princess. If I was lucky enough to have the Princess I would have all I ever need, happiness all wrapped up in a Princess package. It would be like all my Christmases and winning the lottery everyday come all at once if I was fortunate to have the Princess.

Having the Princess in my life already as a friend is already a blessing and a beautiful gift but to have her as that special someone would be a dream come true.

My Christmas wish,

Is this,

Santa,

I've got my list,

What's on it, you might have guessed,

Got it in early to ensure I'm not missed!

But anyway, I'm gonna tell ya!

It's 1st December,

So I'm gonna tell ya!

I'm getting in early,

So hopefully you don't forget me!

Santa, I've been a good boy,

So please bring me the one thing that will bring

me joy,

Santa, I don't want no toy,

Santa, I don't want clothing,

Santa, what I want will make my heart sing,

Santa, I don't want sweets,

Santa, what I want makes my heart skip beats,

Santa, I don't want video games and DVD's,

Santa, what I want gives me butterflies,

Santa, what I want makes me go weak at the

knees,

Santa, what I want, I would love and cherish
forever,
We'd always be together,
Inseparable,
Santa, what I want is adorable,
Santa, what I want would make me smile,
Santa, what I want would make the wait
worthwhile,
Santa, what I want is sweet and lovely,
Funny and bubbly,
Santa, for what I desire,
Is what I'd forever treasure,
For Santa, what I yearn for,
Is the girl that I adore,
For Santa, for Christmas,
Please bring me the Princess,
And her, I promise,
I will love and cherish,
And to her I will pay homage,
So please Santa make my Christmas wish come

true,

I beg you,

For the Princess would be the greatest gift of all,

I wouldn't want nor need anything more,

So Santa, I beg thee,

Please bring the Princess to me.

A Prayer Was Answered

No. 36

The thirty sixth poem in this book for the Princess inspired by songs that remind me of her is inspired by Take That's "Pray".

I chose this song because it reminds me of something that I do every night … pray! Every night before I go to bed, it may sound stupid but I do it anyway, every night before I go to bed I look out of the window and up to the heavens and pray. I say a prayer for the Princess. I ask the man upstairs to look after the Princess and watch over her and keep her safe. I ask him to send a departed loved one of mine to be the Princess' guardian angel to watch over her and keep her safe. I ask him to let me have a wonderful dream about the Princess, it sounds daft I know but it works, I've had many a wonderful and beautiful dream about her. I thank him for all the wonderful dreams I've had in the past about her too! I thank him for every moment spent with the Princess telling him I cherish every second with her and admittedly I ask him if he could see fit for me and the Princess to be together, I know, I know, it sounds so stupid right? But I do it. I promise him that I would look after her and would never let her down so hopefully, he answers my prayer and how lucky I would be.

This girl is so special and I'm willing to give anything a go, praying, dreaming, wishing upon stars, you name it I'll do it except seemingly tell her face to face how I really feel, how stupid huh?

Last night as to the world I said goodnighty,

I looked up to the heavens,

And prayed to the Lord Almighty,

It was only a matter of 60 seconds,

But to the Lord I said a prayer,

For the girl for whom I really care,

It's just something I do every night,

Praying that she will be alright,

Praying that he will take care of her,

The Princess, to which I refer,

I asked the Lord to give me sweet dreams,

And it seems,

That prayers are answered,

The illusion they're not – shattered,

For I dreamt about her not once but twice,

Which was very nice,

Some will say it is just coincidence,

But I don't believe in such incidents,

I said a prayer,

And he was there.

The Princess Prayer

No. 37

The thirty seventh poem in this book for the Princess inspired by songs that remind me of her is inspired by Aretha Franklin's "I Say A Little Prayer".

Well this one isn't really a poem as such as the title suggests, it's a prayer.

As I referred to in the previous poem every night I say a prayer for the Princess, well here it is – this is pretty much the prayer that I say every night. It probably seems and sounds daft but I do it anyway. It may vary slightly but this is pretty much it.

As I said in the previous poem, every night I pray that the Princess is looked after and a guardian angel sent to protect her and watch over her. I thank him for all the wonderful dreams I've had about her and every moment spent with her and I always pray for one shot, one chance at happiness with the Princess.

Hope one day my prayer is answered and I get a chance at happiness with the Princess.

Dear Lord,

Up above,

Please Lord, answer my prayer.

Dear Lord,

Please Lord, look after the most beautiful,

Most gorgeous,

Most sexiest,

Most wonderful,

Most special girl in the world,

.... {HER NAME HERE}

Please Lord,

Protect her,

keep her safe,

And let her know that I love her so much,

And that I'd do anything for her,

And would never let her down,

And thank you Lord for every moment spent

with her,

I cherish every second,

Please Lord,

Let me have a wonderful dream about her,

And thank you for all my wonderful dreams I've

had about her in previous sleeps,

Please Lord,

Send a Guardian Angel to watch over her and

keep her safe,

And let her know that I love her so, so much,

And that I'd do anything for her,

Please Lord, send her this kiss,

{Blows Kiss up to the sky}

{Then whispers}

Love you …. {THE PRINCESS' NAME

HERE}

Please Lord just give me one shot,

One chance, at happiness,

I beg you Lord,

And I promise,

I won't let you down,

And I won't let her down,

I promise I will look after her,

Because I love her so, so much,

So much, it hurts,

Please Lord,

I beg you,

Please Lord,

Just give me one shot at happiness,

One shot at a happy fairy-tale ending,

A happily ever after,

I beg you Lord,

Amen.

{sign of the cross]

Thank you.

Wish Upon A Shooting Star

No. 38

The thirty eighth poem in this book for the Princess inspired by songs that remind me of her is inspired by Simply Red's "Stars".

I wrote this after seeing two shooting stars whilst looking out of the window before bed one night, well morning really it was a little after 2a.m as I don't sleep well for not being able to switch off. I find myself often just lying awake thinking about the Princess.

I've mentioned it before in my previous book "Poems for a Princess" how every night before bed I always look out of the window and up to the sky above and make a wish upon the stars, I know it sounds stupid, but I do it anyway and make a wish, I'm willing to do and believe in anything and everything to give me any chance at all with the Princess no matter how remote. I'm willing to believe in anything and everything from the Easter Bunny to the Tooth Fairy to praying to wishing on stars to Father Christmas! Lol.

The above reminds me of something Elvis Presley once said, he followed many faiths and wore many religious symbols like the crucifix cross to the star of David citing the fact that he didn't want to miss out on heaven on a technicality. The situation is different but the general idea of trying anything is the same in me praying and wishing upon stars.

I remember this one particular night looking out of the window doing what I always do - praying and then wishing upon a star when I saw not one but two shooting stars in quick succession, such a beautiful sight and so I made a wish, they do say if you see a shooting star you're supposed to make a wish so I did, I just hope it comes true just like they do in the movies.

Shooting star,

Up above in the sky afar,

Shooting across the dark night sky,

Oh my,

Look at it go,

Putting on a wonderful show,

Burning a trail so bright,

Illuminating the dark night,

I quickly make a wish,

And then swish,

Just like that it disappears,

The sky clears,

My wish I've made,

For the same thing I've also prayed,

I've also dreamt,

I just hope what I've dreamed, prayed and wished

for is meant,

Meant to be,

She and me,

So shooting star,

Up above in the sky so far,

I beg thee,

To grant my wish for me,

Oh please let my wish come true,

Thank you.

Dreams

The thirty ninth poem in this book for the Princess inspired by songs that remind me of her is inspired by Gabrielle's "Dreams".

A pretty obvious song to remind me of the Princess. "Dreams" – yes indeed – it would indeed be a dream come true to be with the Princess. I really do hope that it does turn out like the line in the song "Dreams can come true" oh I do hope my dream comes true and the Princess and I get together.

If the above happened it would be all my wishes and dreams come true, all my prayers would have been answered, all my Christmases come at once, I would have my happy fairytale ending, my happily ever after that I so desperately long for.

I've had so many wonderful happy, sweet and lovely and some tearjerker dreams of the Princess but always with a happy ending and whilst at work I struggle to switch off and constantly think about the Princess as I'm sitting there getting lost in a daydream about her.

The Princess is always in my thoughts, she's always on my mind.

The Princess is my first thought when I wake and my last thought before I go to bed and even then she never leaves my mind as I constantly dream of her.

Yep, I got this love bug bad!

So here's hoping dreams do indeed come true!

Dreams,

In them how wonderful life seems,

For every night,

My dreams are cheerful and bright,

Happy,

Because of she,

My dreams are the best,

My dreams are blessed,

With and because of the Princess,

Dreams of me and her,

Together,

So wonderful,

So beautiful,

I wish I could dream the dream forever,

And wake up never,

Then the alarm goes off,

I scoff,

And it's time to get up,

Yup,

I was having a wonderful time,

Dreaming about making the Princess mine,

Princess, I wish my dreams of me and you,

Come true,

Then I won't need dreams and fantasy,

Because my dreams will be reality,

And me,

So very damn lucky,

And very, very happy,

If my dreams come true,

And I'd be with you,

For Princess,

I'd be truly blessed,

Having all I dreamed of,

Having the girl with whom I'm in love,

Princess, having you,

Would indeed be a dream come true.

Princess – Take A Chance On Me

No. 40

The fortieth poem in this book for the Princess inspired by songs that remind me of her is inspired by Abba's "Take A Chance".

This was always going to be the last one in this book and I decided that because I'm hoping that once the Princess reads the book and gets to here that she'll think it's sweet and lovely and she'll think I will give him a chance – he really does care about me, he really does have feelings for me, he really is serious, he wouldn't spend all that time writing me a book if he wasn't seriously into me, he must really be in love with me. Princess, I am in love with you.

I would give anything for a chance with the Princess, my heart chose her the very first time I saw her. I knew the Princess was special there and then the way she made me feel like I've never felt before, the way she made my heart race, the way she gave me that butterfly feeling in my tummy, no-one else makes me feel like that. Yes, my heart has definitely chosen her and is definitely set upon her.

I do know deep down, well my head knows and has done from the start really that the Princess is well out of my league, she's beautiful, sweet, lovely, kind, funny, clever – she's special, she could have anyone she wanted so what chance do I have really. I mean I can't compete with the other guys out there, I mean I'm just a secretary, I could never offer her all the lovely things she deserves, all I have to offer is love but is that really enough?

Well with that said, it's a good job my heart rules the head though the head might be marginally more sensible lol – but my heart says never give up – you love her so wait forever if you have to.

Yep, so I hope one day for that one chance at happiness, that one shot at a happily ever after, at a fairytale ending with her – I'll continue to pray, wish, dream for the Princess to take a chance on me.

Princess, no more jibber jabber,

Like the song by Abba,

I ask thee,

For you to take a chance on me,

My heart has chosen you,

No one else will do,

To you my heart belongs,

And so, to reveal,

How I feel,

I've written you another book of poems inspired
by songs,

Songs that remind me of you,

I hope the poems tell you what I wish you knew,

That being that I'm in love with you,

At first glance,

One would say I've got no chance,

But in the name of romance,

I'm going to give it a go,

And you, I'm going to try and show,

Just how much you mean to me,

And so, this is another book especially for thee,

Hope, no matter how small,

I'm going to give it my all,

Princess,

I confess,

I know at first glance,

I don't have much of a chance,

Realistically,

With thee,

But me,

Well you see,

My heart,

From the start,

From when we first met,

On you has been set,

It won't listen,

To reason,

It believes in romance,

It believes I have a chance,

My head,

Says don't be braindead,

She's too good for you,

Deep down I know it's true,

I know you're way out of my league,

But the "what if" fills me with intrigue,

It's stupid I know,

But I've got to give it a go,

Like I said, thee,

I know you're too good for me,

I mean look at you, you're beautiful,

The most beautiful girl in the world, its
indisputable,

You're smart,

You have a beautiful heart,

You're sweet and lovely,

Funny and bubbly,

Elegant,

And intelligent,

You could have any guy,

So why should I even try,

To them I can't compare,

To be fair,

Why should I even bother,

You, I have nothing to offer,

I'm not blessed with looks,

Or mega bucks,

Me,

I'm just a secretary,

And you, in your career, you'll go far,

You'll be a Solicitor or Barrister,

I couldn't offer you all the nice things that you
deserve,

So, to even try to woo you I've got a nerve,

They say God loves a tryer,

So, I'm gonna play with fire,

And take a chance,

By trying to show you some old-fashioned
romance,

By writing you poem after poem,

In the hope of showing,

You, Princess, that you girl, I absolutely adore,

You, I'll do anything for,

You, I worship the ground you walk on,

Princess, you're the special one,

Infinite amounts of love is all I can offer,

And the promise of being true to you forever,

So, Princess I beg thee,

In the name of romance,

To take a chance,

A chance on me,

And let's see,

If there is something beautiful for you and me,

A fairy-tale ending,

That is what I'm dreaming,

So, Princess let's see,

And I ask thee,

To take a chance on me.

Printed in Great Britain
by Amazon